REJOICE, PRAY, GIVE THANKS

Katie Furr

ISBN 979-8-89112-629-9 (Paperback)
ISBN 979-8-89112-630-5 (Digital)

All biblical citations were taken from the New International Version of the Holy Bible.

Covenant Books
11661 Hwy 707
Murrells Inlet, SC 29576
www.covenantbooks.com

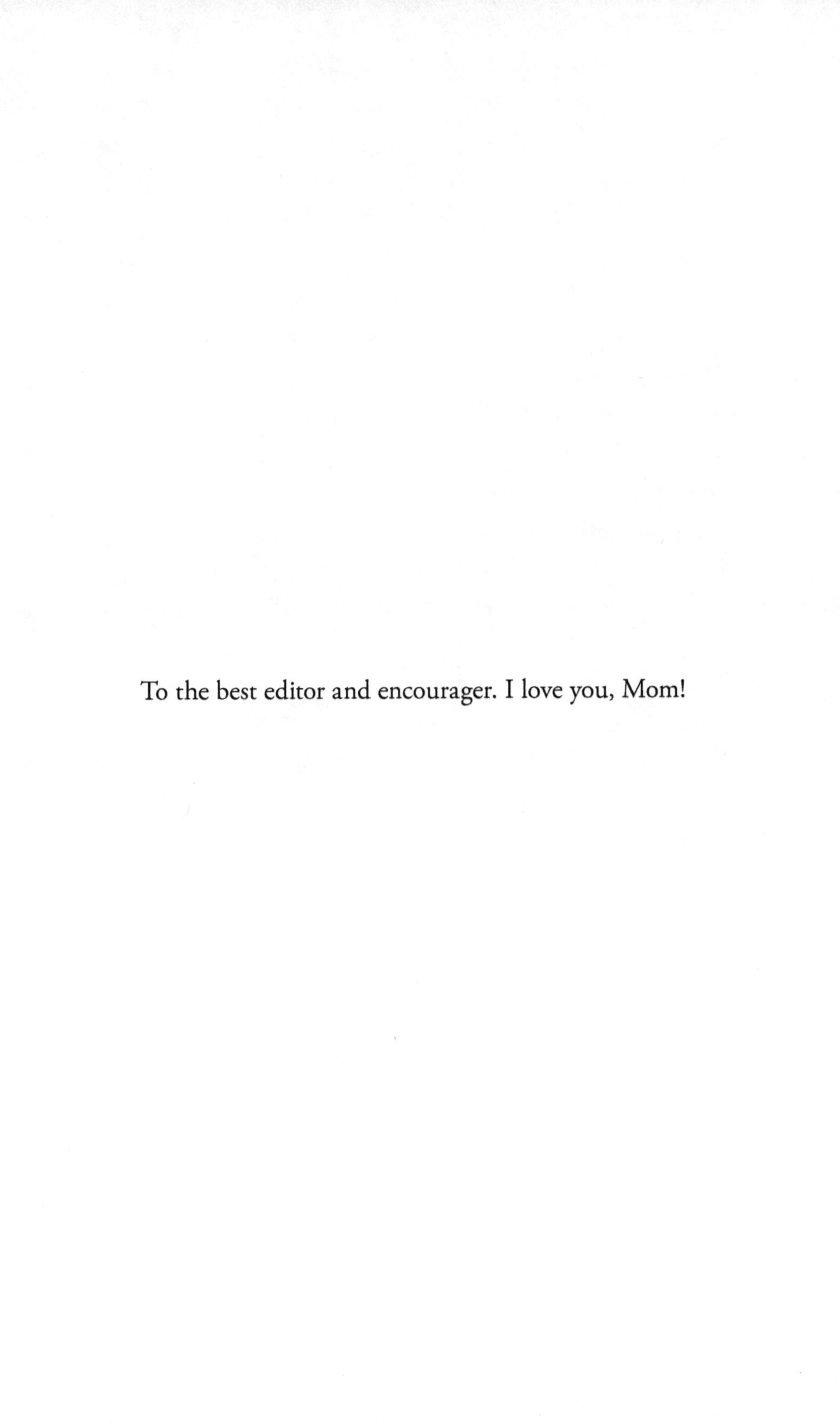

To the best editor and encourager. I love you, Mom!

Welcome! What an honor it is to be on this quest with you for rejoicing, praying, and giving thanks! I have to tell you the story (that definitely includes some humor) that led to this study. I was a high school principal (who is not even five feet tall), you know it was funny to see me walking the halls with all of those teenagers! Before the 2020 school year started, our administrative team worked hard putting many measures in place with the hopes of keeping as many students and teachers as healthy as possible in light of the pandemic. In the days leading up to August, I found myself having a weird forced, almost cringing, half smile on my face as I worked to be positive. I knew this would not work for five minutes after the ring of the first bell to start the school year. I found myself wondering what I should replace my anxious thoughts with and fully embrace. I found a wooden piece of artwork with one of my favorite Scriptures painted on it from 1 Thessalonians 5:16–18: "Be joyful always; pray continually; give thanks in all circumstances, for this is God's will for you in Christ Jesus."

After buying the piece and reading through the verses, I recognized the need for increased thankfulness in my life. Try following my crazy logic; this is where the humor comes in: I thought about how lucky people were during the time of Thanksgiving because they were able to focus on gratitude. It then occurred to me that I could start having my own "thankful Fridays" when I would focus on all of the things for which I was thankful. I wonder if the Spirit said to the Lord at that point, "Give her a minute… It takes a while for this one to catch on." After a few thankful Fridays and reading those verses again, the light bulb *finally* went off—yes, comprehension does take a little longer for some of us! My default setting could and should include a great deal of rejoicing, prayer, and thankfulness! A weight was lifted in my heart, but I had work to do to get there.

A good bit of what I learned on this trek is outlined in this study. You can do this on your own or with others. Each day contains devotional thoughts and scriptures. This book is yours. Feel free to highlight, take notes, etc.! There are questions for reflection at the end of each week that you can also review with others. I pray this blesses you incredibly and that you are able to share what you learn with those on your path. There is *so* much freedom given when we choose a mindset that is focused on rejoicing in our Savior, prayer, and gratitude. May you be rewarded through this journey!

—Katie

CONTENTS

REJOICE!

WEEK 1: WHAT DOES IT MEAN TO REJOICE?

If you are in mourning and truly having a hard time experiencing joy due to grief, that is an important part of this life. Our Savior understands. You may want to start with the prayer section of this study, move on to thankfulness, and end with rejoicing.

Day 1

Welcome to the first day of practicing the art of rejoicing for a solid month! And hopefully not for just one month but for the rest of our lives. It seems that rejoicing should come naturally. Do you rejoice continually? No? Me either. This is something that we are going to have to practice; it's something we're going to have to work at so that it becomes a natural part of our mindset. So be ready to actively participate. Nearly every day of this study, you will be asked to stretch yourself in specific ways. This is definitely a very interactive study; if we want to cultivate habitual rejoicing, we'll have to be ready to work hard over the next four weeks. I pray that this study blesses all who participate, no matter the season of life.

Philippians 4:4 says, "Rejoice in the Lord always, again I say rejoice." *Oxford Languages* says that the meaning of *rejoice* is to show or feel great joy or delight. We are going to start strong with the practice of rejoicing. Stop now and think about how you feel when you experience great joy or delight. Have you ever been told to "fix your face"? Practice "fixing your face" so that you are showing that joy or delight. Do you feel lightness starting to seep in?

Paul, the writer of Philippians, doesn't stop with rejoice only; he says to rejoice *in the Lord*. Ask yourself, why would *you* rejoice in the Lord? Has He done something for you? Is He doing something for you now? Will He do something for you in the future? Take a deep breath and consider what is keeping you from rejoicing. We will practice this further, but for now, lay it in God's hands. Practice the following because we want to experience what is possible through this gift right from the beginning:

- Give yourself actual permission to lay down what hurts, what is difficult, what is so uncertain. Don't lay it down just anywhere! Pray and lay it down at *His feet*.
- Once you have laid it down, think about His goodness and
  - something that is true,
  - something that is honorable,
  - something that is just,
  - something that is pure,
  - something that is lovely,
  - something that is commendable,
  - something that is excellent,
  - something that is worthy of praise (Philippians 4:8).

Now, as you are thinking on our Lord, our Savior, our Prince of peace, our Hero, and these things, allow yourself to *smile*, not just a little smile, but one that is *huge*! Go ahead; it's just you. Get that smile out!

Okay, the next step? Yell out a big "Yes!" If everyone's still asleep in your house, whisper it *loud*!

Are you like me and have wondered why the big "Yes!"? Have you prayed for a friend's child who is struggling and they have a huge breakthrough? Have you heard wonderful news about someone expecting or adopting a child who has waited for so long? Has someone you loved gotten that job they will be awesome at doing, and they let you know? Did you feel like shouting with joy? Yes! God is always moving. We have someone Who is so powerful. We have a King who has already won.

Sometimes, life's circumstances are so difficult that the "Yes!" can only come from the fact that we know this world is temporary and from the knowledge that He is preparing an incredible place for us.

"My Father's house has many rooms; if that were not so, would I have told you that I am going there to prepare a place for you? And if I go and prepare a place for you, I will come back and take you to be with me so that you also may be where I am" (John 14:2–3).

Thank you, Jesus! Receive the gift of reading Revelation 21:22–25. Go ahead; this world is too difficult not to hold onto this glimpse of heaven.

Let's go back to the fourth verse of Philippians chapter 4. There are three key parts:

- Rejoice
- in the Lord
- always.

Always? That seems a little extreme, right? Can I be candid for a minute? Some of us are living like this world is our home. Some of us are living as if this is the end of the line. We are not believing that in this brief journey, God is refining us and those we love. We are not living like we know this is a stop on our way to spend eternity with Him. If we are brutally honest, some of us are comfortable with this world as our home. Some of us are scared of what comes next. It's okay to acknowledge that! Ask God to help you with that fear; He gives good gifts to those who love Him.

So what will you do about "Rejoice in the Lord always" now? This study is about changing our mindset to reflect the attitude of Christ. He loved. He rebuked. He believed. He did not worry. Wow! If the Word tells us to rejoice in Him always, we're probably going to need a few reminders during the day. You may want to set an alarm to go off a couple of times a day that reminds you to rejoice. You may want to write out a verse and tape it to your laptop as a reminder, you could write REJOICE on a piece of paper and put it on your fridge— you could do one or all of these—whatever works! We don't want to go through a Bible study and be the same person on the other side, right? *Do something to help you remember to rejoice.* Take some time to do it now. Becoming a person who habitually rejoices is not something that you will regret.

Day 2

I hope rejoicing made a difference in yesterday. It can be a challenge at times, right? We're going to cover a big part of rejoicing—practicing through song. Let's take a look at these verses from the Psalms:

> But let all who take refuge in You be glad,
> Let them ever sing for joy;
> And may You shelter them,
> That those who love Your name may exult in
> You. (Psalm 5:11)

Before we sing, notice that we need to take refuge in God. We need to seek Him for our guidance and protection. Do we allow ourselves to do this during the day? When we are faced with difficulties and challenges, we must practice going to Him, asking Him for help, and *allowing Him* to work instead of forcing our own agendas. Take time to practice that process today: Pray. Wait for Him to work. Give Him the space to do it. As we wait and are able to watch Him work, we will then feel like rejoicing in what He is doing. Practice it today and rejoice when He moves in His perfect timing.

"Sing to the Lord a new song; Sing to the Lord, all the earth" (Psalm 96:1).

This is interesting because it says to sing something *new*. God is in control and is working for our good continually. We have to be on the lookout for evidences of Him at work. As we see them, we need to sing to Him about them—to let Him know that we are thankful for specific ways in which He is working. If we are doing this, our song will always be new because it will be current about details He is working out right then. These verses also talk about the earth actually singing to the Lord. On your drive today, or your walk, whenever you are outside, take time to see how the earth is uniquely formed by Him and how it is constantly changing. It appears that God likes change! That can be an issue for us, but life would certainly be boring if things never improved, if people never grew, if there were never challenges to overcome. Overcoming the comfort of habit opens a door to spiritual growth. Remember as you sing to Him, this world is not it. He is preparing us for eternity.

"Sing for joy in the Lord, O you righteous ones; Praise is becoming to the upright" (Psalm 33:1).

Has anyone ever told you that something was a "good look" on you? That's what this verse is saying: Praise is a good look on those who are walking in the Lord. So take the time to sing for joy. Praise God in conversation with others; let them know about the wonderful things he is doing. Remember, it's a good look on you!

We've talked about singing a good bit today so take some time to practice it. You can do this any time—while driving, taking a shower, getting ready for the day, etc. If you need a good worship song, I love Rend Collective's "Joy." Check out their lyric video and follow the words. Sing out to the Lord. Do it daily. It will go a long way to help instill in us an attitude of rejoicing.

Day 3

Today we're going to take a further look at what Scripture says about having and gaining an attitude of rejoicing.

"Glory in His holy name; Let the heart of those who seek the Lord be glad" (1 Chronicles 16:10).

We are actually supposed to take great pleasure in the holy name of Jesus. How do we do that? I like to think about the type of person He is based on what I read in the Bible. He was never afraid to love the shunned in front of others. He took on my sin and gave me everlasting life. He cuts to the core of human pride. He gives attention to the outcasts. Take a minute to make your own list. Our Lord is our true hero; the second part of the verse says that we should seek Him and be glad. This world is tough. Where are you seeking the Lord in it? I find Him the most often when I answer His call to serve others. Guess what? When I'm serving I find that I am glad. Think through the ways you find Jesus day in and day out. He calls us to be unselfish and to love the Father with everything that is in us. It's not an easy road, but it is one that is walked in honor. What a Savior to rejoice in!

"His master said to him, 'Well done, good and faithful servant. You were faithful with a few things, I will put you in charge of many things; enter into the joy of your master'" (Matthew 25:21).

I love it when Scripture is very direct in showing us something; this verse certainly is. Jesus is telling a parable here. What does He tell us will happen when we are faithful and responsible with things we are given? We will be put in charge of many things, and then what? We can enter into His joy! Wow, have you experienced this? Have you been faithful with something He has given you? Not holding so tightly to it that you do what you desire only, but that you seek Him and His guidance for what He would desire in it? I've done it both ways, there is *so* much joy when you allow room for Him to work in it. There is no pride at the end because you know that was Him moving through it; all there is left to do is to rejoice because the motives are pure, and you were able to see His hand in it. Practice doing that today. What has He placed you over? Think through how

Jesus would want you to handle what you have been given. Pray to God for guidance in it and for His hand to move powerfully through it. Stand back and allow that to happen. I pray you do this and see the tremendous blessing in it! Your faith will be strengthened by this process!

"But let the righteous be glad; let them exult before God; Yes, let them rejoice with gladness" (Psalm 68:3).

Ever need permission to feel good about being joyful? Here it is! If we are living righteous lives, we should be rejoicing before our God and with gladness! So live today with gladness. You don't have to wear fear, dread, sadness—actually, none of that is what we are called to take on. It's why Jesus told us not to fear so often; He knew it was an easy default setting for humans. We're going to have to work at rejoicing. How will you work at it today? How are you going to remember? You don't want to be the same person you were on the other side of this study. Ask God to help you rejoice in Him, set a reminder on your phone, tape a message on your laptop; work for it to get the reward. He wants you to have it!

Day 4

"Rejoice always" (1 Thessalonians 5:16).

Welcome to day 4 of this first week. Today, you will be providing the content.

Think back to a time of major rejoicing in your life.

- What was happening?
- What are some of the sounds, smells, people, places that are involved in that memory?
- Why do you think you felt so joyful?
- As you've gone through this week, what has brought you joy?
- How have you remembered to rejoice?

First Thessalonians 5:16 says to rejoice *always*—not just when we're excited or happy always. Take time to write out a prayer to God asking Him to help you continue to rejoice in Him and to place it in your mind throughout the day. Also ask Him to reveal to you what is holding you back from rejoicing.

Day 5

Welcome to the end of week 1! The end of the week is supposed to be easy, right? I'm actually going to hit you up with a challenge that will help us going into next week.

"Love does not rejoice in evil, but rejoices with the truth" (1 Corinthians 13:6).

We need to be honest with ourselves about our thoughts and conversations. It is strange to think that we could be wrapped up in the things of Satan more than the things of God even while we are trying to be followers of God. It is imperative that we understand where our thoughts are lying—our thoughts are going to lead us to rejoice or they're going to lead us to very dismal places. We have to choose the truth of God over the lies of Satan because Satan works hard to keep us from a life of joy.

A major truth I was just reading about is found in John 8:51 where Jesus said, "Very truly I tell you, whoever obeys my word will never see death." Seriously, is this actually true? Remember, *this is not our home.* We cannot live like this is our permanent address. We are on a purposeful journey, one that will shape and mold us to be with our Savior. As followers of Jesus, we are walking one another home! We've got to rejoice and spread light so that we will remember that.

Another powerful truth is found in John 16:33 where Jesus also said, "I have told you these things, so that in me you may have peace. In this world you will have trouble. But take heart! I have overcome the world." He is telling us to have peace because He has overcome—we either believe it or we don't. What do our thoughts, conversations, and actions say about our beliefs? Are they weighed down continually in the "that's so sad, that's so scary, I can't imagine"—is there room for this? Yes, absolutely. But waaaaay too often, we let the conversation and our thoughts end there, and Satan gets a foothold. Who is more powerful than anything we are facing? Our God and our Savior! We have no idea how He is working a situation for good. We can share that thought when we are talking to a friend in difficulty. We can think about that *truth* when we see something that is very challenging for ourselves or for someone else. Do we become incredibly tired and sad when those we love turn away from Him? Yes. Can I tell you something that may help? God has not finished writing their story. Even if their story on earth has ended, only God and Jesus knew their mindset and what they were facing. *God is so much bigger than our brains can comprehend.* Is that something to rejoice in? Absolutely! Can we practice rejoicing in the challenges and in the unknown? Yes!

As you get ready for this day or the next, set an alarm on your phone to go off each hour. No, you don't have to do this for the rest of your life—but it may be beneficial for a while. Label the alarm "Rejoicing or despairing?" When it goes off, take a second to think: In the conversation, the thoughts, the actions I am participating in right now, what am I doing? Am I rejoicing, or am I actually despairing over something leaving no room in my mind for God to work through a situation? This is a workout, but you've got this.

Take a few minutes to listen to one of my favorites, "Fear Is Not My Future" (radio version) by Maverick City Music featuring Brandon Lake and Chandler Moore. This song does a beautiful job of voicing some of what we have talked about today. God wants us to grow. Rejoicing actually boosts our growth! May we learn how to fully accept and embrace it.

Week 1 Reflection

We've looked at two scriptures this week that say to rejoice always (Philippians 4:4 and 1 Thessalonians 5:16). Why do you think it is important enough that the command is to "always" rejoice?

What do you see is the importance of not just singing a song to the Father, but singing a new song when you communicate with Him?

Think about a time you have seen a person rejoicing, and then think about a time someone was despairing. List the differences in what you witnessed. What is the difference between despairing and grieving?

What new thoughts, feelings, or discoveries have you experienced with regard to rejoicing this week?

End your time asking God to help you see what you need to change and how to best go about that in order to rejoice more.

❦

WEEK 2: WHAT'S HOLDING ME BACK?

Day 1

Welcome to week 2! As we work through these four weeks on how to rejoice, the hope is that our mindsets will be molded so that the act of rejoicing will come much more naturally in our daily lives. In order to make that happen, we need to put in some work to discover some things that may be holding us back from rejoicing. This week will be challenging, but progress will be made that can benefit us in this area for the rest of our lives if we will allow it. Take a moment to pray that God will help us see what needs to be mended and that he will open many doors throughout this week.

Throughout our lives, we develop habits. Some of these are very healthy like caring for ourselves and others well, and being responsible with what God has given us. Of course, some habits are harmful to us—doing something unhealthy when under stress, like not engaging in Bible reading and prayer, or spreading gossip. Satan, the father of lies, knows how to separate us from hope.

Take a look at Romans 15:13: "Now may the God of hope fill you with all joy and peace in believing, so that you will abound in hope by the power of the Holy Spirit."

That's a lot to digest! First, we have a God of hope. That's beautiful to think about, isn't it? He's not a God who can't be trusted or Who loves for bad things to happen to us. He is our heavenly parent Who has hope for us. He is always at work. This verse says that

God can fill us with joy and peace, but there is a condition. Take a look at what it says after "joy and peace"—"in believing." We have to take that next step—we have to believe in order for our God of hope to fill us with joy and peace. When we are engaged in holy habits, we demonstrate faith and belief in our God of hope. When we are engaged in bad habits, it is our outward display of hearts that actually don't fully believe. Is that statement taking it too far? Take a minute to think through an unhealthy habit you have—maybe it's listening to music that definitely doesn't reflect God, reading books that have content that lead you away from thinking on what you should or not engaging in church. Pinpoint that unhealthy habit you have for just a minute. Does the activity you engage in show that you believe in a God of hope? Does the habit fill you with true joy and peace? We have to dig deep to decide if we are willing to replace that habit for one that actually does lead to joy and peace. We have to go ahead and identify what we are going to do spiritually rather than defaulting to possibly years of something else we have been doing. It's going to take work. So are you ready to work to change for the better?

There is reward in the work of believing. Look at the second part of the verse: "so that you will abound in hope by the power of the Holy Spirit." Have you ever done that? Have you ever said, "Okay, God. I don't see how you're going to work through this, but I believe in you and I'm going to live so that my actions reflect that." Try it. Today when something comes up that would normally drive you into an action that reflects unbelief, *stop* and *think* about what default thought pattern or action you're about to engage in next. Choose to believe and give God room to work. Wait for joy and peace; I can tell you it's come to me when I've chosen to do this. The power of the Holy Spirit that comes and fills me with hope is incomparable with anything I have sought to fill myself with that is from this world. Does it take work? Yes. Do I have to place reminders around me like verses where I can see them to help me to this? Yes. Do whatever it takes. As children of God, we are not of this world. Whatever we turn to that is from this world is *never* going to fill us, and we *will not* change from the person we are now. When we turn to God for power and choose to believe—the joy, peace, and hope that come are incredible because He is what we actually need. So choose to do the work. Ask God to give you strength. Place reminders where you need them. The reward is real, and it is priceless!

Day 2

I hope you were able to pinpoint some habits that may be getting in the way of experiencing true joy in God. Take a minute to read through the following verse about Jesus:

"And though you have not seen Him, you love Him, and though you do not see Him now, but believe in Him, you greatly rejoice with joy inexpressible and full of glory" (1 Peter 1:8).

Jesus should be our hero, right? We are told that we should be His disciples—that we should have the same attitude as Him and that our walk should mirror His. Something that gets in the way of our joy may be a misunderstanding of our Hero that we don't even realize we have, or it may be a lack of connection with our Savior. We know that He loves us, and we know that He is preparing a place for us. Should we have a relationship with Him? Should we think on the things that He wants us to do? Should we recognize times when we feel closest to Him? Yes, we should. Turn to John 17 and read Jesus's prayer for His disciples and those who believe in verses 6 through 26.

Take a minute to continue thinking about our Savior. He goes after the outcast, He heals those who are sick and hurting. He is not afraid to say what needs to be said, He puts the self-righteous in their place—Every. Single. Time. That's someone I can get behind. He is also someone who I don't think I reflect on enough. He's our Commander, our Prince of peace. He is calling us to go to battle for Him each day on this earth until we get to eternity with Him. We can take joy in following this leader, right? So think about Jesus today. Take some time to truly realize the magnitude of following Him and competing on a spiritual battle ground that He's already won. He wants us to help bring many more souls to Him. What a joy, what an honor, this is something major to rejoice in!

Day 3

Today we're going to zero in on *what* we're thinking about and *how* we are thinking throughout the day because our thoughts can keep us from or lead us to rejoicing. Today is going to take some concentration!

Psalm 33:21 says, "For our heart rejoices in Him, Because we trust in His holy name."

Our hearts rejoice in what/who? In Jesus. Why? Because we trust in His holy name. Remember back to yesterday, we were talking about our Savior and the need to truly know Him. We've got to know Him in order to trust Him. And we're going to have to release the tight hold we have on our life and give it to Him. Otherwise, are we really trusting Him with anything? This requires a huge shift in our mindset. So let's practice.

Ask God to lead your thoughts about things that need to be accomplished today. Give your God and Savior your world and your day to deal with; ask for wisdom, insight, courage, and love in going forward with what They need you to do. Ask for clarity in what you need to do to please Them. Ask for the desire to want God's will above your own.

Now, go ahead and list the things you need to accomplish today. Pray. Ask God to move powerfully through the day. As you move through the day, leave space for Him to order your day, even if it means it all turns out much differently than you anticipated. We do not determine the outcome when we are trusting in Him.

Now, write out the things that are bothering you, causing you anxiety, things that you are uneasy about. Put a check mark by areas you actually have control over. Ask God to help you see what you need to help with and what you need to leave in His hands. As you pray, visualize yourself actually handing over this list to our Lord. Feel the weight lift as you let it go.

When we are handing over our days and the things that cause us concern (that we actually have zero control over), this requires trust. We're letting go of whatever we thought we had control over, and we're asking to be God's servants in whatever ways He sees fit.

We're becoming better followers of Jesus, "For I seek not to please myself but Him who sent me" (John 5:30). We're seeking God's will for our daily lives, for those we love and whatever future to which He is calling us.

This is going to take belief. We are going to have to *practice* believing that He is sovereign, that He knows much better than we do, and that we can trust Him to hand over lives to and even our desires. When we believe and do that, it takes a *ton* of weight off of our shoulders. When we can trust that the great I Am is in charge (who will give us much better gifts than we imagined), and that we don't have to manage the outcome because it is all in the hands of an incredible God—there is so much *joy* to be found! I promise that there is peace and that your heart will rejoice in Him when you do this! The more you make this a practice, the more God will reveal His power in your life. Praise God for His wonderful ways and for our awesome Savior!

You may want to set a reminder on your phone to go off a few times over the coming days for something like the following—pray, give it to God, trust, and rejoice! Remember, we are not in charge of the outcome. It may look totally different than we thought it would. Let it go, observe what he is doing, and rejoice. Take a few minutes to listen to Travis and Lily Cottrell sing "What a Beautiful Name." I pray it blesses you as you seek to rejoice in Him.

Day 4

"So they went on their way from the presence of the Council, rejoicing that they had been considered worthy to suffer shame for His name" (Acts 5:41).

When I think of rejoicing, the word "suffering" does not quite match in my mind. What about you? We have all suffered in different ways and to different degrees. This is part of life, right? When you think back to something you suffered, can you think of the ways it helped you to grow? Can you think of something you later rejoiced over because of suffering you experienced? I think we all can. Suffering shame for His name, that is a high calling. There are some who suffer more than others. We see the incredible faith of those who were true martyrs in Scripture; there are people around the world who suffer tremendously today.

Has He called you to do something and you suffered some shame or embarrassment while doing it? I imagine each of us has in different ways. If we feel led to do something in the name of Christ, we need to be ready to suffer. Read that again; if we feel led to do something in the name of Christ, we need to *be ready to suffer*. It is part of it. Think back to some of the stories of your favorite heroes you remember from the Bible. Take a look at Hebrews 11 for a blessing. Come back to this after you have finished reading.

Pay attention to the last five verses. *They suffered.* How and why did they do this? They knew their current circumstances were temporary, but their future was in God's hands. We have spiritual opportunities; choosing to use our time for these opportunities may very likely not be convenient or comfortable. We have to ask ourselves some soul-searching questions if we are going to experience rejoicing in the midst of suffering:

Are we willing to truly accept that we have a home waiting for us that is better?

Read Hebrews 11:1. On a scale of 1 to 4, with 1 being iffy, and 4 being concrete, where is your faith in this promise?

Do we love those around us enough that we will have the courage to point to this when we suffer?

Read Hebrews 11:8; do we believe in our Lord enough that we are willing to step up to something He is calling us to do?

Some of the most beautiful verses in the Bible to me are found in Hebrews 11:13–16:

> All these people were still living by faith when they died. They did not receive the things promised; they only saw them and welcomed them from a distance, admitting that they were foreigners and strangers on earth. People who say such things show that they are looking for a country of their own.

These people *believed*. They stepped out in their faith. Pay attention to the next two verses because they show that even if we believe and step out, there will still be choices to make:

"If they had been thinking of the country they had left, they would have had the opportunity to return. Instead, they were longing for a better country—a heavenly one."

This is where the rejoicing comes in:

"Therefore God is not ashamed to be called their God, for he has prepared a city for them."

Can you imagine? When we are stepping out for Him, He is not ashamed! He is preparing something much better! We can live in mediocrity. But guess what? When you're running to get the prize (1 Corinthians 9:24), the rejoicing is *so* much greater! If you are suffering right now due to stepping out for something He has called you to do, rejoice in that! You are among the greats who did the same. You are not alone! If you have been holding back to answer His call, what are you waiting for? Get after it, He is ready to help you. And remember—you *will* suffer. When you do, make the decision to rejoice!

Day 5

Think through what/who we are taught to rejoice over. We are to rejoice in our Lord. There are also other areas we are to rejoice over. Take a look at Luke 10:17–20:

> The seventy-two returned with joy and said, "Lord, even the demons submit to us in your name."
>
> He replied, "I saw Satan fall like lightning from heaven. I have given you authority to trample on snakes and scorpions and to overcome all the power of the enemy; nothing will harm you. However, do not rejoice that the spirits submit to you, but rejoice that your names are written in heaven."

Jesus is sending out His followers. They are excited over the power they have been given to drive out demons. But Jesus cautions them about *why* they rejoice. There is an interesting point to be made here. If we are truly committed to Him and advancing His Kingdom, God will be able to move in powerful ways through us. Jesus makes a vital point with His followers. We are to rejoice in what is coming. There will be no room for *our* pride in anything that God is doing through us. Truth be told—He can do it with or without us! We are to keep our focus on the Creator and what He is doing, this is where the rejoicing comes in.

Take some time to think about something incredible you have witnessed someone else do for the Kingdom. Did you rejoice more over the circumstance than who and what was behind it? That's an easy thing to do. Jesus is telling His followers to keep their focus on the prize that never disappoints. He works in many ways through us. We will see some fruit when we have chosen to step up for Him, much fruit will come that we will never know about.

Take some time to ask the Father to reveal something you are rejoicing over that is insignificant compared to His glory and what He has planned. When we are serving with the right perspective, what we rejoice over never disappoints!

Week 2 Reflection

Throughout this week, we have covered areas that may hold us back from rejoicing. I hope the following questions are beneficial in reflecting over what we've studied.

How have you made progress this week in overcoming a habit that may keep you from rejoicing? What have you replaced the unhealthy habit with?

How have you made more of a connection with Jesus this week?

How have you allowed more room for God to move in your life and in the lives of others this week?

How has your thinking on suffering been affected based on what we studied?

What have you found that you actually rejoice in? If it is not something of God, how can you change this?

⁞

WEEK 3

Some How-Tos

Day 1

We're now halfway through our study on rejoicing! I hope you are making progress as we work to change our mindset in following this command. This week, we will talk about some basic how-tos when it comes to rejoicing. This will involve a lot of participation on your part. My words will be fewer, and your practice will be more involved.

> Glory in His holy name;
> Let the heart of those who seek the Lord be glad.
> (Psalm 105:3)

> Blessed be the God and Father of our Lord
> Jesus Christ, who according to His great mercy
> has caused us to be born again to a living hope
> through the resurrection of Jesus Christ from the
> dead. (1 Peter 1:3)

One of the best times to rejoice is when we begin in prayer. We are talking to God and rejoicing in His Son and in what God is doing. This is important to our Father. As we start to pray, we can acknowledge and proclaim who He is and the things He has done. For example—Holy Father, God over all, Great I Am, Giver of every perfect gift. Then take time to thank Him for specifics—what He is doing, who He has sent into your life, fruits you have seen develop. Remember, we need to be purposeful and intentional with rejoicing. It is a command that has been given to us. Of all the times that we should be rejoicing, shouldn't it be when we are communicating with the Creator?

Today, most of the words will come from you. Take time to write out a prayer acknowledging who our Father is. Look up the names of God and the scriptures that connect with them. Then let Him know that you are rejoicing because of what He is doing. Be specific in the gifts He is continually providing—not only for yourself but for those around you. As you identify these gifts, be sure to think of those that are eternal—the fruits of the Spirit are a great place to start. Sometimes we have to remember that it's not about us; we are rejoicing in God and in our Savior. May you be blessed as your mindset switches from thoughts of yourself to thoughts of our Father and as you rejoice in Him in prayer.

Day 2

"But about midnight Paul and Silas were praying and singing hymns of praise to God, and the prisoners were listening to them" (Acts 16:25).

What a powerful scene—Paul and Silas, jailed in shackles and chains, decided to sacrifice what were probably very anxious thoughts by choosing to praise God in song. This is probably my favorite way to rejoice; I bet it is for many of us. When the babies are young in the nursery, we quickly start teaching them songs like "Jesus Loves Me." It is amazing how young they are when their hearts pick up the words and tunes to the songs they are learning. God is already planting a seed of joy in their souls for Him!

God instructs us to sing. He created us and knew singing is good medicine. It lowers anxiety and activates parts of our brains linked to emotion. Take time to read Ephesians 5:19–20 and Colossians 3:16. Praise God that even as we praise Him; He is blessing us! We are truly fearfully and wonderfully made!

As I get older, I find that I could not be more thankful for Christian music. There are three Christian stations set on my car radio that I bounce between often. When I was in my early twenties, someone challenged me to listen to Christian music. I really didn't know a lot about it and thought it was strange at the time. They convinced me to try to listen for a week. It did take a minute, but it has been one of the biggest gifts of my daily life! Think about some of the songs in which you are truly rejoicing and praising God when you sing. Then take a few minutes to sing your favorites. Concentrate on releasing praise and rejoice to the Father and to the Son as you sing. Below are a few of my favorites if you need something to get you started.

- "Joy of the Lord" by Rend Collective
- "Rejoice" by Andrew Ripp
- "God really loves us" by David Crowder and Dante Bowe

Day 3

> How beautiful on the mountains
> are the feet of those who bring good news,
> who proclaim peace,
> who bring good tidings,
> who proclaim salvation,
> who say to Zion,
> "Your God reigns!" (Isaiah 52:7)

This is such a beautiful verse! Do you rejoice about God to others? I think some of us do, from time to time. But I bet we could be *a lot* better at it! How do we even start without being someone no one can relate to? Do you keep notes on your phone? I do. If not, you might carry a small pad of paper to write things you need to remember. The assignment today is to take note of good news you can rejoice to others about. You may have to set a couple of reminders on your phone to go off during the day for this one. Even if it's just one piece of information a day that can change not only our own outlooks, but those with whom we come in contact. Secondly, practice picking up on someone else's good news and rejoicing over it. Link it back to it being a gift from the Father.

There are many things that take life without giving a good return, but rejoicing is life-giving. This is something that will take effort; it is also something that can become a habit that will be powerful in determining what our minds are marinating in. Would you want a marinade that is bitter and smells horrible? That seems like a ridiculous comparison, but no—I wouldn't. God doesn't intend that for our brains either. He created our minds to feed on creativity, beauty, and excellence. Take care; we are the only ones who can determine if we are sources of rejoicing or sources of negativity. Ask the Father to help you see the good; there is so much to rejoice over and to share with one another.

For further thinking on this, check out Benjamin William Hastings and Blessing Offor's "That's the Thing about Praise." It is such a good one!

Day 4

"I rejoice at Your word, As one who finds great treasure" (Psalm 119:162).

This verse is pretty clear—we are to rejoice at His word! And to rejoice as though we have found a great treasure. Why? Because that is what it is! Have you had trouble reading a passage before? Yep, I do sometimes. Every once in a while, the Bible can be difficult to understand. Personally, I cannot take on too much reading at once. I usually read a passage that is contained under the heading that often appears in a chapter of the book I'm reading in my Bible. Before I start to read, I pray and ask God to help me visualize and understand what He is trying to show me in that passage. After I read, I think about what I've read and try to apply it to an area I need to know and grow through. I may write out a phrase or verse that really stuck out to me. Then I will pray again and ask God to strengthen me through what I've read and learned. That's it. It's different for everyone; you have to find your own groove.

Some people love studies; some love to look up meanings of words in Hebrew (language used for the Old Testament) or Greek (language used for the New Testament). Some people read passages three times, some like to highlight, others listen to the scripture (I really like to do this when I'm tired). It takes time to develop what works best for you. Find what it is because there is treasure that's revealed if you are eight years old, or if you're eighty.

A friend of mine loves to say that Scripture never comes back void, it is never empty. Sometimes, I do have to pray that I will hunger for the Word. It's just fine to ask God to help you to want to study what He has given. He wants us to search and find the gifts that are found in studying it. Practice this now. Choose a book of the Bible, choose a few verses, pray and ask God to bless your reading, and look for the treasure. It's priceless!

"The kingdom of God is like treasure hidden in a field. When a man found it, he hid it again, and then in his joy went and sold all he had and bought that field" (Matthew 13:44).

Day 5

"His master said to him, 'Well done, good and faithful servant. You were faithful with a few things, I will put you in charge of many things; enter into the joy of your master'" (Matthew 25:21).

Take a few minutes to read Matthew 25:14–30. Jesus is very purposeful in telling us that gifts are given with, what I believe, the intention that They are used for the Kingdom. Verses 28 through 30 can be difficult to read, but they are important. Otherwise, they would not be included. Each of us has been "loaned" gifts. God gives us the freedom to decide how those loans are to be used. Go back and read verses 20 through 23. The end of verses 21 and 23 say, "Enter into the joy of your master." There is joy to be found and rejoicing to occur when we are using and multiplying our gifts for His service. I've done it both ways, I've used my gifts for the course I chose, and I've given my course to Him for my talents to be used for the mission He chose. In the course I chose, I was in control, and I predicted the outcome. I found that even when the desired and predicted outcome occurred, the joy was limited, the feeling was shallow and there was little substance to it. When giving over the talents He gave me for His service, I found that at first the path didn't make complete sense to me. As I journeyed, I couldn't predict what was going to occur. This made me lean on Him more. It helped me to discover what it meant to not worry because He was in control. The end of a journey with God in the lead is so much more profound. There are events that occur that I never thought possible, I was not dictating the day—He was.

When I choose to be on His journey, I wake up to take on what He is giving me to do that day with the gifts He has given me. The weight is on His shoulders to carry because that is where it belongs. When I realize I don't have to carry the weight because it's not mine, the joy found in the journey is so much greater. In the end, there is much rejoicing in my God and Savior because it is clear that they are the ones who made it happen!

So try it. Try it throughout today. Try it with your next big project. Try it when looking toward the future. Are you willing to give up your plans and dreams for what He has planned for His mission? *The outcome will be so much better!* You can trust Him. Start by asking Him to help you to desire to be on His path rather than on your own and to believe that whatever He has planned is going to be so much greater than anything you could ever want!

Week 3 Reflection

This week, we covered some "how-tos" when it comes to rejoicing. May you be blessed as you reflect on the week!

How do you find it most comfortable to adore God and rejoice in Him in prayer?

When do you enjoy rejoicing most through song?

Why is it important to rejoice over Jesus and the Father with others in conversation?

Have you found a way that is more effective for you to study the Bible?

What is a talent you have that you have not used for the Kingdom up to this point? Spend some time in prayer asking God to help you see how to best use this talent for Him.

⚜

WEEK 4

Rejoicing Every Day

Day 1

It's the last week of the Rejoice study! I truly hope this study has helped to transform your mindset. It can be challenging to keep digging during the final days. Pray that God will reveal ways to help you rejoice this week, and that He will instill in you a desire to do so.

This week, we are tackling rejoicing in the daily grind. If it is to become a go to for our brains, rejoicing needs to be habitual.

"Therefore, having been justified by faith, we have peace with God through our Lord Jesus Christ, through whom also we have obtained our introduction by faith into this grace in which we stand; and we rejoice in hope of the glory of God" (Romans 5:1–2).

This is an excellent verse for starting the day. Being *justified* by faith means we are *made right* in the sight of God by our faith. He sees us. We must have faith that he is in control, that Jesus is the only way to the Father, and that They love us incredibly. If we wake up knowing we have been justified by our faith, this verse is saying that we have peace; we are right with God through Jesus. Praise Jesus for His incredible grace!

Jesus died for us and made it possible for us to have peace with God. If there is something holding you back from having this peace with God, ask Him to help you work through it. I have found that I have grieved a situation and did not understand the reason God was allowing it, but I also know that He is the only one who can work through it and somehow bring beauty from terrible circumstances. (Verses 3 through 5 of Romans 5 shed some light on how God works through trials.) Seek out solid, reliable counsel from a minister or Christian counselor if you are blocked from peace. Give yourself grace in working through your emotions. God created us, and Jesus lived on this earth and felt the struggle; they know our limitations. Move toward that peace. God is moving; it may not be in the way we would, but in His perfect timing and way.

Accepting and acknowledging God's sovereignty and gaining the peace that "passes understanding" (Philippians 4:7) is a huge spiritual gift. It makes it possible for the last part of this verse, "and we rejoice in hope of the glory of God" (Romans 5:2). He gives hope. He gives hope when there is none. He gives hope and life in situations that seem impossible. Have you met someone who praises God in the middle of great difficulty? Have you met someone who was literally rescued by God? Have you met people who make it their daily mission to love like Jesus? There is real hope, and we can have it as we rejoice in God's glory.

This is not our world, it is not the home we are longing for; however, there are plenty of people on this planet spreading the truth about Jesus, pouring hope into situations that change the trajectory of not only someone's day but their life. Will you decide each day to look for opportunities to spread hope? Will you purposefully rejoice in the God who makes hope possible and in the Son whose grace enables us to stand? If you start having trouble during the day, ask someone to pray for you; ask God to show you His majesty and splendor so that you can rejoice. So let's go! There is an entire day ahead to rejoice in our God and Savior. Others are counting on seeing this in us. Let's point the way to Him. Place a verse near where you're getting ready for the day. Go ahead; do it! Start your day rejoicing in the *peace* and *hope* we are given. These gifts are eternal and are far better than any gift this temporary world could offer!

Day 2

> Let all who seek You rejoice and be glad in You;
> Let those who love Your salvation say continually,
> "The Lord be magnified!" (Psalm 40:16)

> Glory in His holy name;
> Let the heart of those who seek the Lord be glad.
>   (1 Chronicles 16:10)

When we read through these verses, we can see that we have to be intentional about rejoicing because of the word "seek" used in both of these passages. One of the best ways to be purposeful in rejoicing is choosing a time of day to do this. It can be done in a few different ways. I like to set aside the time I'm driving to work as time to worship and rejoice by listening to praise songs. It can be done in nature. If you enjoy taking walks each day, you may want to choose a lunch break to focus on rejoicing. This can also be done as you are getting ready in the mornings. Go ahead and plan a time that you want to devote to rejoicing each day. Commit to doing this. As you rejoice, be glad, magnify the Lord, and glorify His name. This time is both a gift to God and to ourselves. Lay down other thoughts and tasks and spend this time rejoicing in the Lord.

You may want to enjoy the gift of listening to Dante Bowe's "Joyful" during your time.

Day 3

> Rejoice with those who rejoice.
> (Romans 12:15a)

> "In the same way, I tell you, there is joy in
> the presence of the angels of God over one sinner
> who repents." (Luke 15:10)

Think about the last time you truly rejoiced with someone. I have a friend who does an incredible job with this. I know that if I call her with good news, she is going to say my name loudly and quickly follow with praising God for what he has done. She has taught me so much through the ways she openly does this. I, on the other hand, have to work at this. Knowing the effect it has on me for her to acknowledge how good our Father is, I see how important and beautiful it is to do this. She is also just as enthusiastic when someone leaves a sin behind. Do you ever wonder why we might hold back from rejoicing? Is it the anxiety of knowing that we may be in a good moment now, but that a hard moment is coming? Is it because we actually don't really care enough that someone we love is rejoicing or that someone has turned away from sin? These are questions we should be asking ourselves. If others "will know we are Jesus' disciples if we love one another" (John 13:35), rejoicing with them and praising God when people turn to Him should be strong indications of our love, right? So let's practice. Be yourself! Express your joy in your own style—a word, a hug, a handshake, a card—we can all express joy in unique ways. Let's pray, asking God to help us to be aware of when we should be rejoicing with others. Let's be on the lookout for it today. Do you need a reminder? Sometimes I might tie a string around my wrist or wear a piece of jewelry I don't normally wear to help me remember to be more attentive. Do what works, but don't miss out on the gift of openly rejoicing with those who we are with on this journey!

Day 4

Today, we're going to think through our responses in rejoicing during the difficult times that do come. Take a minute to pray and ask God to reveal to you how you can best grow in this area and then read through the verses below.

> Rejoice in hope, persevere in tribulation, be devoted to prayer. (Romans 12:12)

> Though the fig tree should not blossom And there be no fruit on the vines, Though the yield of the olive should fail And the fields produce no food, Though the flock should be cut off from the fold And there be no cattle in the stalls, Yet I will exult in the LORD, I will rejoice in the God of my salvation. (Habakkuk 3:17–18)

> Rejoice and be glad, for your reward in heaven is great; for in the same way they persecuted the prophets who were before you. (Matthew 5:12)

> Beloved, do not be surprised at the fiery ordeal among you, which comes upon you for your testing, as though some strange thing were happening to you; but to the degree that you share the sufferings of Christ, keep on rejoicing, so that also at the revelation of His glory you may rejoice with exultation. (1 Peter 4:12–13)

In every difficult circumstance that people were experiencing over two thousand years ago, the act of rejoicing was still commanded. Tribulations, famine, persecution, and fiery ordeals *are not new*. The difficulties we experience *are not new*. Remember that we are on a journey that is molding us and shaping us. The most growth we will have will be through major challenges in our lives. You can count on that.

Take a minute to read these verses from John 11:25–26: "Jesus said to her, 'I am the resurrection and the life. He who believes in me will live, even though he dies; and whoever lives and believes in me will never die. Do you believe this?'"

Now read from John 5:17: "Jesus said to them, 'My Father is always at his work to this very day, and I, too, am working.'"

So if we believe and act on our faith, we never die, and God and Jesus are *always* working. If we believe in these profound truths, we have more than enough reason to rejoice! We need to; facing life's trials is no easy task. The people around us need to see our example of rejoicing to know the right perspective to have in good times and in bad. Do we mourn and grieve in difficulty? *Yes*, but our difficulty is not the end of matters, so our mindset should not dwell in a state of sorrow.

What if the next time we or those we love are in a major trial, we condition our brains to think of the following:

- Hard times are promised to us.
- This is part of our walk here.
- I'm going to trust in Him and have joy because Jesus is with me to help me.
- This is the temporary life He's called us to.
- He's refining us for eternity with Him.

Write the verses and the parts of this statement out that you most identify with and place it somewhere you easily see it daily. Trials are a part of our lives. Satan would love for you to believe that situations cannot be redeemed. Don't give in and live like that! Ask God to help you believe. This isn't the end; there are wonderful experiences waiting. Live rejoicing in our God and Savior!

Day 5

Best for last, right? Yes! Save the best for the last part of your day. This is a time we have to claim for the Lord's. He has been working throughout your day. So when you get ready for bed; think of how you have seen God's hand move during that day—how you have seen Jesus move through someone else or even yourself. Ask God to help you recall times that He has worked that day. Read through the following verses:

> Rejoice in the Lord always; again I will say,
> rejoice! (Philippians 4:4)

> For You, O Lord, have made me glad by
> what You have done,
> I will sing for joy at the works of Your hands.
> (Psalm 92:4)

This is the mindset we need to have. We need to practice rejoicing and singing for joy at the end of the day. So how will you remember to do this? I place a couple of objects on my bedside table that help me remember to reflect on this. Because guess what—if I don't, then I won't. You might try a scripture card, a cross, a heart—whatever helps!

I pray that you have seen how intentional we must be in rejoicing. I pray that your mind has developed patterns to quickly go to praise when you see God moving and to rejoice because even though you may not see something physically happening on this earth, you know God's and Jesus's powerful hands are at work. I pray that you work on your relationship with the Father and with Christ through prayer and reading Scripture so that you will have this to also rejoice over. We have so much more ground to cover in prayer and thanksgiving! You've got this! Enjoy TobyMac and Blessing Offor's "The Goodness" as we close and rejoice!

Week 4 Reflection

This week, we have concentrated on what rejoicing looks like on a daily basis. I hope you are already seeing results!

What is the best way for *you* to get into the mindset of rejoicing as you rise in the morning?

What time of day works well for you to take time to rejoice? How do you do this?

Who is someone you know who steps up to rejoice with people? How can you picture yourself rejoicing with others?

What is an area you've had to work on during this study in trusting God and knowing He wants the best for you? How have you worked through this?

What is healthy about praising God at the end of the day? What specific reminder can you use to help make this a habit?

PRAY

WEEK 1: THE BASICS

Day 1, The Lord's Prayer

I hope the Rejoice study has blessed you and that you feel a deeper sense of awareness and longing for the eternal while having a more defined view of what we should be doing while we're here.

Let's look back at verses 16 through 18 from 1 Thessalonians 5: "Rejoice always; pray continually; give thanks in all circumstances, for this is God's will for you in Christ Jesus."

Over the next two weeks, we are going to focus on prayer. We are going to look specifically at what Jesus had to say about it. Please stop now and ask God to grow our hearts and minds in this area.

Verse 17 does not just say to pray, it says to pray in *all* circumstances. Think through a typical day. We get up, have breakfast, interact with family or roommates, dress, go to work, socialize with others, and then come home. It's not usually that simple, is it? There are more complex things that happen. Someone gets upset, you remember a bill that is almost late, a coworker is struggling, you've got that thing you said you would help your friend plan and you're not quite ready, the phone rings, and there's an emergency you were not expecting—the person you care for is on your mind as they battle illness. The list could be very long. There are plenty of circumstances to pray through; we just have to remember to do it!

Let's take a look at what is probably the most famous prayer. Read Matthew 6:9–13 and then come back to this. Jesus shows us that we should first honor the Father. I really love to do this when starting a prayer. We are speaking to the Creator, the Great I Am. He gives us the gift of being approachable. When we first acknowledge who He is and praise Him, we are starting with the right perspective. Look at verse 10. Before asking for anything, Jesus says that we are to ask that His Kingdom come, and that God's will, above our own, is to be done. This is us saying that we are submitting our wants and desires to His will: that the way *we* want a situation to work out is nothing compared to what *He* is doing. I love verse 11! It is about today only and is a basic request for sustenance. Verses 12 and 13 close the prayer with asking for forgiveness—as much as we forgive others—and deliverance from evil. Some late manuscripts of the Bible include "for yours is the kingdom and the power and the glory forever. Amen." Once again, Jesus shows us to end as the prayer begins, giving praise to our Father.

Below are some outline headings to help you form a prayer as Jesus instructed. Practice writing out a prayer in this format and then pray through it to the Father. Just so you know, most of the time I write out my prayer in a bulleted format before I pray—it helps me to get my mind in the right place and to then concentrate. I pray that you are blessed through this exercise.

- Adoration of God
- Giving our will in exchange of His (be specific if needed)
- Daily requests
- For forgiveness (try to be specific), and for an attitude of forgiving others (be specific here as well)
- Protection from evil
- Adoration again and closing

Day 2, In Jesus's Name

In John 14:13, we see Jesus talking about prayer: "And I will do whatever you ask in my name, so that the Father may be glorified in the Son."

We have to really search out the heart of Scripture to understand it, right? It would be easy to stop with the first half of verse 13, right before the comma. That's not where Jesus stops, though. If we are remembering that this world is not it, that we will not die, and that we are being prepared for a home with Him, we are living with an eternal mindset. What comes after that comma in verse 13 is a big deal, "so that the Father may be glorified in the Son." Think about it. Is what we are asking actually bringing God and Jesus glory? Some situations are so deep and impactful that it is hard to think that what we ask would not bring Them glory. Remember, only God knows the ins and outs of every situation. Only God knows what is going to bring the most glory in the end.

In. The. End. When we are praying, we do not know the end, right? If that is the case, how do we know what to pray? What if that job is not the right fit? What if that relationship will lead to some serious damage? What if God wants to redeem a situation in ways that we cannot fathom and in ways that we won't see? Remember, God is the great I AM. He is working in ways that we cannot see, and sometimes in ways we *won't* see or understand, and we've got to make peace with that, even with the circumstances that break parts of us.

Several years ago, on a journey to better know what to pray when I had no clue, and how Jesus would do "anything" when asking in His name, I sought to understand what the "anything" was in His name. I thought about how He wants us to be, the qualities He talks about us having in Scripture. So obviously the big one is love, right? Loving God with everything we have and loving others as ourselves is something that glorifies God and is how Jesus told us to live (Matthew 22:34–37).

Another way that I have seen Him work powerfully is by praying for the fruit of the Spirit in any situation. Jesus told us that the Spirit would be our helper, so we can trust the fruit that comes from a life lived by the Spirit. The outcome of the situation may be completely different and worse than I want or desire, but—I am not God and do not know the intricacies of the details He is working through, nor can I fathom the outcomes in which He is best glorified. The fruit that comes from the Spirit totally alters mindsets in any situation and, I have found, brings hope. When I pray for this fruit over someone going through a circumstance and/or for myself, I have seen Jesus's work powerfully through it. If someone is blessed with love, joy, peace, patience, kindness, goodness, faithfulness, gentleness, or self-control (Galatians 5:22–23), that is going to be a blessing. I believe that is also God being glorified.

So try it. Take some time to pray now. Instead of asking for a specific outcome, pray for a person and yourself to be filled with the Spirit and for specific fruit. Take the time to look at the person, or yourself, as they go through the circumstance to see if you can see Jesus working in that way. We are on a journey, God is molding us, and He has sent us a Helper (John 14:16–17). The help is free! It's ours for the taking, ask Him for it and prepare to be tremendously blessed by it.

Day 3, In Secret

"But when you pray, go into your room and shut the door and pray to your Father who is in secret. And your Father who sees what is done in secret will reward you" (Matthew 6:6).

Do you have a place where you like to pray? A specific place where it is just you and God? Notice in this verse that Jesus tells us to specifically do three things:

- Go into your room.
- Shut the door.
- Pray to your Father.

It is obvious that we are not to make a spectacle of prayer, but I think there is also something deeper to these instructions. Perhaps Jesus wanted us to experience privacy with our Father. The Bible says that "Jesus often withdrew to lonely places and prayed" (Luke 5:16). Why do we meet with just our best friend for dinner or coffee? Why is it important for a married couple to have time to talk together alone? Why are important meetings behind closed doors? A connection needs to be made, and there are important things to discuss that are not everyone's business. Going to a place of seclusion is also important for concentration. What you discuss with God is your business; it is important enough that it be a closed-door meeting. It is not for the display of others; this is solely time for the Creator and you. It is so easy to think that we are not important enough to even think about having a conversation with the Father. Jesus knew better, and it was important enough that He gave us specific instructions including the how and where of praying. Is this something that is intimidating to you? It has been to me at different times. It can be easier to pray with a group of people to the Great I Am. Remember, God is our Father. He is a Father who gives good gifts and who loved us enough to sacrifice His own Son. He wants to hear from us. This holy connection is important.

What did Jesus say the result would be? "Your Father…will reward you." We have to remember that our mind does not work the same way as God's does. What we receive may be totally different than what we expect. So we need to keep our eyes open for the reward. For me, it is a lot about the connection and relationship I have with Him. I know I can be honest with Him because He already knows what is happening. He fills me spiritually and provides peace when I give things over to Him. I do not have to worry because my Father is in control.

Take a few minutes to try this. If you're not already in your room, plan for a time to be there later today; close the door and pray to your Father. Then look for the reward. Keep seeking; keep knocking. He is there.

Day 4, Pray against Temptation

"Watch and pray that you may not enter into temptation. The spirit indeed is willing, but the flesh is weak" (Matthew 26:41).

Even Jesus, *even Jesus* was tempted by Satan. He *knows* the feeling. He can empathize, and that is why He has the authentic credibility to tell us to pray to not enter into temptation.

Read James 1:14–15: "But each person is *tempted* when they are dragged away by their own evil desire and enticed. Then, after desire has conceived, it gives birth to sin; and sin, when it is full-grown, gives birth to death."

Evil desire…temptation…desire conceived…sin…death.

Jesus knows we will be tempted. He knows giving in to temptation can lead to death. Therefore, He is *very* aware of our need to watch and pray. *It is okay to ask God to take away a desire to sin.* Sometimes, I think we are scared to let God know that we are struggling with a temptation or sin. News flash—He already knows! And in my experience, He has helped take away my desire when I have asked. Jesus knows the power behind praying to God. Did you know that He is there beside God relaying our messages to the Almighty? He is pleading on our behalf!

"Who is he who condemns? It is Christ who died, and furthermore is also risen, who is even at the right hand of God, who also makes intercession for us" (Romans 8:34).

He loves us enough to do this! So be honest—with yourself and with your Creator. We don't want death, right? We need to be truthful enough with ourselves to look at the death our sinful desire has the ability and probability to bring if we allow Satan a foothold. We need to do what Jesus said: Watch and pray that we will not enter into temptation. *This is important.* He came so that we would have life. Resist the lies of the evil one and recognize spiritual death when it is knocking on your door. Go to our Father, He is there to protect you. If you read a little further in James 4:7, you read the end of the story when you follow the steps Jesus gave: "Submit yourselves to God. Resist the devil, and he will flee from you."

Praise God for His faithfulness! Take some time to be real. Pray to God about what is tempting you. He wants you to turn to Him; He wants you to have life.

Day 5, Your Turn

Spend today in prayer. Practice using the following outline that has prompts from this week included.

- Go into your room.
- Shut the door.
- Apply the following prayer guide.
  - Adoration of God
  - Give over your will in exchange of His (be specific if needed).
  - Daily requests
- Pray for you or someone else who needs prayers to be filled with the Spirit; pray for specific spiritual gifts or fruit to be granted to yourself or the person for whom you are praying (faith, hope, love, joy, peace, patience, grace, mercy, etc.), for forgiveness (try to be specific) and for an attitude of forgiving others (also specific). Also pray for protection from evil.
- Pray against temptation (be specific).
- End with adoration again.

Week 1 Reflection

Did using the prayer guide on days 1 and 5 help you to pray? If so, how did it help and how might you want to use something similar as you go forward?

How did reading through day 2 change your perspective on John 14:13?

Where and when do you find you like to pray most? Why do you think that is?

Why do we not want to pray to God about what is tempting us? What makes it easier to do this?

WEEK 2: GOING
DEEPER

Day 1, For Our Enemies

"But I tell you, love your enemies and pray for those who persecute you" (Matthew 5:44).

Wait, what? Yes, that is what Jesus said. But we may already be letting God know how they have hurt us. Why would we go to Him and ask for healing for ourselves over something they have done and then turn around and lift them up to the Father? Can we actually create healthy boundaries and still do this? Yep. What if we thought about how God could actually work in their lives? We need to get to a place where we want this for them because that's love, right? Is it alright to ask God to help you want His best for them? Of course it is. Talk openly to God about your struggle.

Notice that Jesus did *not* say, "for those who persecuted you"—it is present tense. That means we're to pray for them while the persecution is happening. Wow. That takes a very strong individual. I'm thinking that means Jesus knows we have the strength to do it. Does He truly understand that we are human? Read Hebrews 4:14–16:

> Therefore, since we have a great high priest who has ascended into heaven, Jesus the Son of God, let us hold firmly to the faith we profess. For we do not have a high priest who is unable to empathize with our weaknesses, but we have one who has been tempted in every way, just as we are—yet he did not sin. Let us then approach

God's throne of grace with confidence, so that
we may receive mercy and find grace to help us
in our time of need.

He was here, experiencing human emotions. People did terrible things to Him. At one of the darkest moments, while Jesus was on the cross, He prayed, "Father, forgive them; for they do not know what they are doing" (Luke 23:34). We are His disciples; that means we follow Him and pattern our actions after Him, not just when it is a bit of a challenge but also when it is downright hard. If we are going to sing songs like "I belong to Jesus" or "I surrender all," then we need to mean it. May we mean it when we're praying, especially for our enemies. If you are facing some enemies, be obedient, be brave, and take the time to pray for them.

Day 2, Straight to the Point

"And when you pray, do not keep on babbling like pagans, for they think they will be heard because of their many words" (Matthew 6:7).

Yes! My favorite! Are there some things Jesus said that you can really get behind? This is it for me! It probably has more to do with the fact that I struggle with concentration. I also love for people to get to the point. Some would say "Amen!" to this and some would think that is a bit rude. At any rate, Jesus did tell us not to babble. Have you ever told God what was going on in a situation and said something like, "He's in the hospital because he was in a terrible accident and now his wife is scared and his kids are trying to come as quickly as they can." That all may be true; the ironic part is that God already knows what's happening, right? Or have you been asked to pray in a public setting and you wanted to do a great job with the prayer and maybe added in some Bible verses or some eloquent words but actually had little thought about praying to the Father? This is more of what Jesus is talking about. Have you ever been humbled by a beautifully simple and sincere prayer? I bet God loves those. When we can be ourselves and also recognize that we are communicating with the Creator and praise Him for it, when we are to the point because we know that God is already in the situation, and when we ask in faith, we are being transparent with our God. He does not need a show; He wants our heart, soul, mind, and strength. Try concentrating on what you want to bring to His throne; honor Him as you approach and submit to His plan. May you be blessed as you pray!

Day 3, Throughout the Night

"One of those days Jesus went out to a mountainside to pray, and spent the night praying to God" (Luke 6:12).

I would think that a few people reading this have experienced praying throughout the night. I most remember doing this as the parent of a teenager a few years ago. I could see a battle for my daughter's heart and mind and felt a great need to go to God on her behalf throughout that evening and into the early morning hours. Jesus shows us by His example that there are times to do this.

Have you ever felt very uneasy about a situation you or someone you loved was facing and continued waking about it throughout the night? Those are usually the times when it is a golden opportunity to take it before the throne. Have you ever been a part of a prayer chain that woke you in the middle of the night because of an emergency occurrence? That is the time to pray to the Father. Sometimes I wonder if God tires of hearing from me. With the amount of praying that Jesus did and the specific ways He told us to pray, I don't think that is the case. You may need to write out a verse to have near your bed so that you will remember to go to God before sleeping or so that if you are having trouble, you will know to pray. We are God's children, He loves us. Place a reminder somewhere close to where you sleep or to where you go when you cannot so that you will remember to go to God whenever that happens. Going to God in prayer throughout the night for a special need is a privilege. Sleep can come later!

Day 4, Jesus's Prayer

> My prayer is not for them alone. I pray also for those who will believe in me through their message, that all of them may be one, Father, just as you are in me and I am in you. May they also be in us so that the world may believe that you have sent me. I have given them the glory that you gave me, that they may be one as we are one: I in them and you in me. May they be brought to complete unity to let the world know that you sent me and have loved them even as you have loved me. (John 17:20–23)

It is so beautiful to me that we actually get to read what Jesus was praying to God. Take a moment to soak that in. Before He was crucified, these are some of the words that He prayed to God. And they are about *us*. He is praying for us. What is He asking? That we be *one*. I don't know about you, but that is a bit of a kick to my gut. Of all the things Jesus prayed for us, it was for us to be unified. If we are His disciples, should we be concerned about the things that He was concerned about and prayed over? Should we pray about them? I know that I have not spent nearly enough time praying that we would be unified so that the world would know that God sent Jesus and so that all would know that God loves the world just like He loves Jesus. Wow, I don't know about you, but I need to concentrate on praying about this. I need to pray about this just like I would pray for those I actually know and love. I need to care enough about others in this world that unity with my brothers and sisters in Christ is more important than any personal opinion about something that is not spelled out in Scripture. Please join me in praying for unity and for the world to know that God sent Jesus because He loves them just like He does His Son. If it was important enough for Jesus to pray, it should be to us as well.

Day 5, Your Turn

Spend day 5 in prayer. Practice using the following outline that has prompts from this week included.

- Go into your room.
- Shut the door.
- Apply the following prayer guide.
    - Adoration of God
    - Give over your will in exchange of His (be specific if needed).
    - Daily requests
- Pray for you or someone else who needs prayers to be filled with the Spirit; pray for specific spiritual gifts or fruit to be granted to yourself or the person for whom you are praying (faith, hope, love, joy, peace, patience, grace, mercy, etc.). For forgiveness (try to be specific) and for an attitude of forgiving others (also specific). Also pray for protection from evil.
- Pray against temptation (be specific).
- End with adoration again.

Week 2 Reflection

How did reading through day 1 of this week change your view of praying for your enemies?

Do you tend to be a person who can babble in prayer or are you more straightforward?

Have you ever prayed for something throughout the night? What was the outcome?

What was special to you about Jesus's prayer?

How do you think this section may have impacted your view on prayer?

GIVE THANKS

WEEK 1: MEDITATION ON THANKFULNESS

This week is built for you to meditate on biblical gratitude. It is a time for you to fully invest in worship, reading through Scripture, reflection, and prayer. My words will be few during this time so that you are able to dive deep into what needs to be revealed. We will touch back on some of the topics introduced this week as we progress through the study. Stay strong as you are equipped with thankfulness.

Day 1

Read and pray: Take some time to read through 1 Thessalonians 5:16–18 and then ask the Lord to reveal His truth as you work through this day and the rest of this study.

Worship through song: Having a daily attitude of thankfulness is something that is not only possible, it is what we are called to do. It is meant to be a default setting in our minds.

Pull up "Revelation Song" by Philips, Craig, and Dean. Take a pen or pencil and write out the words that stand out to you as you listen. Feel free to jot down thoughts that come to mind as well.

Day 2

Do I have permission to be grateful during any circumstance?

God calls us to live in thanksgiving to Him because He is working powerfully. We arrive at the point of having thanksgiving as our default setting by acknowledging His presence and His hand in everything around us.

Turn in your Bible and read through Psalm 104; make notes below of the majesty of God and what attributes cause gratitude and praise for Him.

Think through the following statements in relation to Psalm 104:

- Our perspective should be impacted by the mighty works of God.
- It is okay to wonder what God may be doing in any situation.
- If our wondering is coming from an attitude of gratefulness, this greatly impacts our perspective.

Day 3

That situation we're just not thankful for…

It is possible to believe God is sovereign over everything and is active, even in circumstances that are difficult for us to accept or understand.

Psalm 107 is full of examples of God actively working in situations of people's lives. Read through this chapter and make notes below of how He works in wondrous ways.

Worship through song: Pull up your favorite version of "It Is Well." As you listen, reflect on how God is sovereign over situations that bring pain. While listening, pray about the circumstances you may be struggling with to be well with your soul, knowing God's hand is in them. Jot down words that resonate in your heart.

Day 4

Q&A with yourself: During a typical day, it might be easy to have an ungrateful attitude when we become stressed. That stressed feeling typically occurs on a normal day for me when these things are happening: Nearly all emotions are traced to love or fear. Someone could make the argument that thanksgiving is a byproduct of love and a frantic or stressed feeling is a byproduct of fear. Do you believe this? Why or why not? During times of the day when I am rushing and it may be pretty difficult to dwell in thanksgiving, what can I do? Normally when someone has done something incredible for you, we do something out of true gratitude for that person as a way of thanking them.

The following are important questions to ask ourselves in light of what Jesus has done for us:

- Am I living in a way that reflects true thankfulness toward Christ?
- What am I doing to regularly help someone who cannot help themselves?
- How can I incorporate this into a regular routine?

Day 5

Take some time to write out a prayer to God considering what you have learned this week.

Dear Father,

You are…

Thank you for…

I confess that…

Please help me…

Please help those I love…

In Jesus's name,

Amen.

Worship in Song: Listen freely to Rend Collective's "Counting Every Blessing." Write out phrases that stand out to you. Allow joy and gratitude to spill over the walls of your heart.

Week 1 Reflection

How does having gratitude as a default setting promote unburdening of weights we shouldn't carry?

What are some of the practical things you could do on a typical day to claim a mindset of gratefulness?

Why would incorporating serving someone on a regular basis who cannot help themselves generate gratitude?

End your time in thanksgiving to God and ask Him to bless you on this journey.

WEEK 2: HE IS LORD, AND I AM...NOT

Day 1

I am excited to start this week with you! During the first week of meditation, we read through the entire chapter of Psalm 107. In this chapter, it is evident that God is intricately involved in the details of growing and molding each of us and everyone we deeply love. (If you have not read through this chapter yet, be sure to—it is truly thought provoking.) Take a look at Mark 10:17–31 and especially focus on verses 29 and 30. If Jesus is truly our Lord, we will be brave enough to give ourselves, and those we love over to Him. It is possible to be deeply grateful to Him through each and every situation. We must truly believe that His way is better than any path we believe is better for ourselves or those we love. If we say that Jesus is our Savior, we must be brave enough to continually trust in Him, even if those we love deeply fall away. There will always be a remnant for His Kingdom and those who belong to Him will be watching to see what we do. May we submit to Jesus today and be brave enough to take up the crosses He has for our lives. May we be grateful for the sacrifice He made, the blood in which we are washed, and the lives we are called to live.

Jesus's calling on my life:

The response I have had to it:

The area(s) in which I need to grow:

Day 2

I hope you all are blessed by today! First John 3:1 says, "How great is the love the Father has lavished on us, that we should be called children of God! And that is what we are!"

We are part of the most elite group on this planet. God's calling is on every single one of us. We are chosen by the King of kings! Praise God that we are part of his army. As those who are called, it is just fine to ask God to help us dwell in thankfulness today. You might even want to set an alarm on your phone for later today to remind yourself to just be thankful.

Before we move on, go back to Psalm 107. Think about a situation that causes anxiety within you. Maybe it is even something that has not occurred—thoughts of losing loved ones, decisions those we love may make, unknown plans God may have for us. Let's work on releasing the situations that are God's, *they are His to handle—let's not fight against it, instead may we learn to praise Him in them.* We can let that situation go from our stronghold and believe that God is over it because the *power of Christ lives in us.* Make the choice to believe that it does. The beautiful part is that God already has the situation in His hands; we just have to surrender any control we think we have over it. How freeing it is to let that circumstance go and have the ability to be thankful to the Father who is constantly at work and loves us so much more than we can fathom!

Take a few minutes to listen to Bethel's version of "It Is Well." May it be well with you, and may gratitude dwell in your heart today.

That situation I need to give over to God:

The reason I may have a stronghold on it:

Prayer of release:

Day 3

During the daily grind, sometimes we forget that God and Jesus are working continually (John 5:17) and that it should be the Great I Aм who is working through us (Philippians 2:13). A powerful start to the day is in expressing thanksgiving to Him—remember to ask Him to help you be filled with gratitude throughout the day and in prayerfully giving our day over to God. Try actually voicing that you are giving the day over to Him. Let God know that it is not yours but His to do with as He wills. When He is the one working through us, it is not our ballgame any longer. We are playing in His game, and He is the one calling the shots.

Read through Psalm 91. Notice the four following verses in this chapter—1, 9, 14, and 15. These let us know we have continual decisions to make in order for our Lord to work powerfully in our lives. He wants to lead us; we can choose to allow the Most High to do this. And then, may we dwell in thanksgiving knowing that His angels are actually fighting battles for our protection that we may never know about! Turn that worship music up loudly today as you go about your tasks, the King of kings is fighting on our behalf!

Spend time writing out the decisions we must make to receive specific blessings based on the following verses in Psalm 91:

1:

9 and 10:

14:

15:

Day 4

Think back over the past year and work to view situations in awe of the many ways God is moving. Have we grown stronger? Hopefully. Do we know what He might be preparing us for? Not really. We do know that for those of us who claim Jesus as our Lord, we should be riding through life on His coattails and not our own—I cannot think of a better place to be! He calls us to a life of love and service; it's not complicated but His message is very clear.

I want to take a minute to talk about my grandmother's sister, Candace. Everyone in my family (my quite colorful family—probably like many of yours) truly loves her. She is beautiful, both inside and out. She has the best laugh; she loves those around her deeply, but not at all in a controlling way which is quite refreshing. When she cries, everyone notices, but she is nearly always up for a good time. Her husband died in a tragic accident over twenty years ago. She stayed beside her oldest son as he left this earth due to cancer. Aunt Candace is strong because of the One on whom she focuses. She is a woman of love and service, and gratitude is evident in the way she is not self-seeking; she is truly a joy to be around. She spreads peace. I honestly cannot remember a word of discontent she has said. She makes me think of this verse from Proverbs 31: "She is clothed with strength and dignity; she can laugh at the days to come."

When our eyes are fixed on what the Lord is doing and hearts are full of gratitude, it is much easier to be this person. May we laugh at the days to come, and may we build up whoever is on our path this week. If it is one person or five, may we view one another in love knowing that God is in control of each of our paths and that all we have to do is sit back and be grateful.

Whose path do I need to view differently?

What is one area in which I need to change my thinking so that I am able to laugh at the days to come?

What steps can I take to get started?

Day 5

May God continue to lead us as we seek to honor Him with grateful hearts. Be sure to take some time to pray before beginning today's study, it will be a challenging one.

When you hear that someone has incredible news of something like an engagement, a new home, a great job opportunity, do you wonder with anticipation of what that experience will be like for that person? It's always interesting to wonder about situations, especially when they seem positive. However, we tend to wonder negatively about tough news—the diagnosis, that disappointing decision, a loss. If we change our mindset to wonder with grateful anticipation of what God may be doing in difficult circumstances, I think we start to become true warriors in His Kingdom. It is easy to wonder only with sadness, frustration, or hopelessness. Certainly the Father knows we will experience mourning and anger, and He wants us to bring our hurt to Him. But if we also wonder in hope, we can wonder in thanksgiving of what He is doing and what He is preparing to do in our lives and in the lives of those we love.

Take a look at Daniel chapter 6. Go ahead and work out your spiritual muscles reading it, then come back to this.

Now that you've read it, take a look at verses 10 and 23. How beautiful it is that in the midst of incredibly difficult circumstances Daniel "prayed just as he had before, *giving thanks* to his God" and that "no wound was found on him because he had *trusted* in his God"! Daniel could have negatively wondered himself into oblivion. It seems obvious he must have wondered in positive anticipation of what God was doing and what He was going to do. In what situation do you need to positively wonder? This action is a game-changer and makes you particularly dangerous to the enemy. Remember, when we finish this study, we do not want to be the same people who began it; we want to be changed for the better in our thanksgiving to God. Is this natural for us? I don't think it is for most of us. Will it take work? Yes, but there are major blessings in it because we will be living in much more of the truth of what God is doing.

Take some time to pray for God to give you the strength and resolve to think courageously about how He is working during difficult circumstances.

Week 2 Reflection

> For this reason I bow my knees before the Father, from whom every family in heaven and on earth derives its name. I ask that out of the riches of His glory He may strengthen you with power through His Spirit in your inner being, so that Christ may dwell in your hearts through faith. Then you, being rooted and grounded in love, will have power, together with all the saints, to comprehend the length and width and height and depth of the love of Christ, and to know this love that surpasses knowledge, that you may be filled with all the fullness of God.
>
> Now to Him who is able to do so much more than all we ask or imagine, according to His power that is at work within us, to Him be the glory in the church and in Christ Jesus throughout all generations, forever and ever. Amen. (Ephesians 3:14–20)

Look back at days 1 and 2. In what area(s) do you feel you need to grow to allow God to have control over your life so that you can truly embrace the freedom of thankfulness?

On day 3, we looked at verses in Psalm 91 that indicate we have decisions to make in order to receive God's blessings. Which of those verses stood out to you?

I wrote about the godly spirit of my aunt on day 4. Who is someone you know whose attitude and actions reveal trust and joy in the Lord?

A challenge of wondering positively of how God may be working during a difficult circumstance was given on day 5. How can this open doors for gratitude?

Spend some time praying for God to continue to open doors next week!

WEEK 3: HIS LOVE
IS GREATER

Day 1

Welcome to week 3! I am praying for each of us to recognize the importance of what we are studying this week. We are seeking to firmly establish gratefulness deep in our roots. We have worked to recognize that the Father is over our lives and the lives of those we love, and that He is continually working because he loves and cares for us so much more than we have the ability to fathom. Over the next couple of days, I pray that our eyes will be opened to the fact that the love that flows from Jesus must be greater to us than our fears.

Take a look at John 15:1–17. Read through these verses and then focus on verses 9–17. Jesus intends for us to spend our time truly loving those in our paths. First John 4:18 is so radical: "There is no fear in love. But perfect love drives out fear, because fear has to do with punishment. The one who fears is not made perfect in love."

When we take the time to truly think about it, so many of our emotions and reactions are rooted in fear or love. Throughout this week, ask yourself if you are experiencing an emotion or are acting/reacting out of fear or love. If it is something that causes anxiousness, it probably goes back to fear. Even during something as simple as being irritable while trying to get a task accomplished, it is important that we ask—why are we irritable? Is it out of fear that we will not have enough time? Why not react in love as we are accomplishing the task? Taking the time to monitor our emotions and reactions will not be easy. Satan would love to make us feel that this is not necessary and does not truly impact our gratefulness. I can assure you that it does and that this is very important to Jesus. If we want to grow to be like Him, like the Father wants us to do, it will take getting out of our comfort zones and believing in His continual mindset of love.

Do we believe in our own fears or do we believe in His love? Honestly, this is what it comes down to because we are called to be His. He has called us to walk in His love—what an awesome place to be. If we make accomplishments in this area, I can assure you that we will be grateful! I'm praying for each of us to have the nerve to do this today!

Think through a time of day you are usually irritable, ask for God to reveal to you the source of your fear or anxiety. Set an alarm for this time on your phone and label it "fear or love?" This will help you remember what your focus is on throughout the week.

Day 2

I pray that God will open our eyes and hearts today. Our Savior continually loves us. We have access to peace from the Prince of Peace Himself. What incredible blessings we have to be thankful for as Jesus's followers.

I believe that part of being grateful for the identity you have in something or someone involves having complete understanding of who or what it is that you profess to belong. To proclaim that we are followers of Jesus in today's world is quite a bold move whenever you look at the Scriptures. Turn to the book of Luke and read through the headings in bold print as you move from chapter 3 through chapter 11. As you look at these headings, think about what they are indicating about the type of being Jesus is and what He truly stands for—this is important because if we say that we are following Him; many of these are callings we are laying on our own lives and the rest are things we say we believe without a doubt about our Savior. Go ahead and take a look, then come back to this.

Chapter 12 brings very comforting words, and it brings words that are quite challenging. Take a look at the following verses and jot down what you notice:

- 4–7
- 14 and 15
- 32–34
- 47 and 48
- 49–53 (perhaps the most challenging)
- Skip over to chapter 14 and lastly read verses 25 through 27.

When we say we are followers of Christ, we are members of a radical calling. In order to say that we are truly grateful, there may be some of his teachings with which we have to come to terms. I certainly have had to do this, but I can tell you that His love and mercy continue to be greater than anything I have on this earth. May we be bold, may we be brave, and we know deep in our bones that His love is great!

Day 3

I hope you are up for today after thinking through and swallowing some of the challenging verses from yesterday, I am encouraged to know that we are on this road together! For those of us who know the Lord, we have to train ourselves to recognize that sometimes in the toughest circumstances, God's love works the most powerfully.

I was blessed to witness what was probably one of the most beautiful displays of thankfulness in the midst of sorrow I will ever get to see this side of heaven. A few months after my cousin married, her husband was diagnosed with cancer. We knew the next few years were going to be very difficult. During one of his surgeries, his mother, my cousin, and I walked down to Starbucks to get a boxed lunch. His mother's presence was and has always been very calming. The three of us were very quiet as we were opening our lunches. She stopped and looked at both of us and said, "I'm thankful. Can we pray?" It was probably the most stunning display of gratitude I have witnessed; it was evident it came from the core of her being.

It was very difficult for me to understand how she could be grateful in that moment. It is through truly recognizing the ways the Lord loves us deeply through difficult circumstances and in the ways that people are often brought to Him through these that we can begin to understand how gratitude is possible. The other huge piece to the puzzle is living in the knowledge of heaven and knowing without a doubt that this is our temporary home. Remembering that we are foreigners here is a very important part of our daily mindset. All of this is for His glory, every single bit of it! Especially in the heartache, God loves us, Jesus is our Savior, heaven is waiting—and we can be truly thankful!

We will never have to wonder if there are others courageous enough to live in this mindset. I've seen it in others and I bet you have too. May we prepare ourselves to be this way if we are not already, we will need to believe in the faithfulness of God and our home in heaven for one another at different points of each other's lives.

Spend some time dwelling on the following verses and ask God to help you develop a deeper sense that this earth is our temporary home.

> Let the peace of Christ rule in your hearts, since as members of one body you were called to peace. And be thankful. (Colossians 3:15)

> Devote yourselves to prayer, being watchful and thankful. (Colossians 4:2)

> Do not be anxious about anything, but in every situation, by prayer and petition, with thanksgiving, present your requests to God. And the peace of God, which transcends all understanding, will guard your hearts and your minds in Christ Jesus. (Philippians 4:6–7)

Day 4

I hope you are blessed today as we reveal a critical part of our DNA as Christ's servants that increases levels of thankfulness in our lives. Have you ever noticed that when you are actively doing the things of God and striving to live like Christ, your mindset is healthier? We know that one of the prominent teachings of Christ is servanthood. I heard someone say that Christ beautifully served those who could not help themselves.

Take a look at Luke 22:14–27. Keep in mind that this was most likely a very emotional evening, Jesus was giving some of the most important information He could leave with those He loved. Words that ring out at the end of this passage are "But I am among you as one who serves."

It is crucial that we realize an important part of our makeup as followers of Christ is to regularly serve those who are truly in need. It is difficult to be selfish, downtrodden, jealous, greedy, etc., when we are actively serving those who cannot help themselves. We are saved from ourselves, and thankfulness naturally surfaces when we establish a regular routine of being personally involved with helping those in need.

I testify that yes, it is very important to give financially, and it is a big part of what we should also do, but there is a massive blessing in stepping out of our comfort zone to personally help others in need. It is beautiful to watch the joy in others who help in different ways such as taking resources to families who may live in government housing, helping people who suffer with addiction, stuffing backpacks with food for students—the list is endless, and it is inspiring!

A few years ago, I felt like this was really lacking in my life. I prayed for God to give insight as to how I could routinely serve, and He did with a children's home. This organization cares for children of incarcerated mothers. Once a month, my daughter and I baked and decorated cookies (Shelby definitely did the decorating), and we took them to the children. Can I tell you that this made a huge impact on my level of thankfulness? We had to take time to think about each month's cookie theme, we spent time going to the store and purchasing supplies, baking the cookies, and taking them to those beautiful children. Engaging in this helped to save me from selfishness.

I really cannot tell you how life changing it is to have a way in which you are personally involved with serving those in need at least once a month. If you do not have this as part of your regular routine, I challenge you to pray and seek out a way to do this. His blessings will overflow in it, and you will be amazed at how your level of gratitude multiplies!

Day 5

> God is exalted in his power.
> Who is a teacher like him?
> Who has prescribed his ways for him,
> or said to him, "You have done wrong"?
> Remember to extol his work,
> which people have praised in song.
> All humanity has seen it;
> mortals gaze on it from afar.
> How great is God—beyond our understanding!
> The number of his years is past finding out.
>   (Job 36:21–26)

I pray that thanksgiving flows out of our hearts as we continue this study and that we will choose to dwell on it in our minds. There were some deep concepts covered this week. If you have not been able to do it yet, go ahead and take the time now to set some reminders or alarms to go off on your phone during the day to be thankful and set a couple to also ask yourself if you are responding out of love or fear. It's amazing how much this can help to bring us back to a mindset of gratitude. Next week, we will finish with a look at some amazing examples of gratefulness from some true heroes in the Scriptures. We are almost to the last week of our study and hopefully to the point of habitually choosing a mindset of thankfulness. There is not one of us who cannot do this; pray for your hearts and minds to be filled with thanksgiving. Praise God, He loves us incredibly!

Week 3 Reflection

> Shout for joy to the Lord, all the earth.
> Worship the Lord with gladness;
> come before him with joyful songs.
> Know that the Lord is God.
> It is he who made us, and we are his;
> we are his people, the sheep of his pasture.
> Enter his gates with thanksgiving
> and his courts with praise;
> give thanks to him and praise his name.
> For the Lord is good and his love endures forever;
> his faithfulness continues through all genera-
> tions. (Psalm 100)

Think back to the fear/love challenge. Did you find that there were times of the day when you were typically more irritable than others? Were you able to find a root cause that stemmed from fear? If so, how has this perspective helped you?

Look back at the verses on day 2. Were there any that were difficult for you to accept? How does knowing that God is working in our lives help you to swallow what is required of us as followers of Christ?

On day 3, I shared about a beautiful display of gratitude. Can you think of a time you witnessed supernatural thankfulness in someone?

How could incorporating a regular routine of service to others promote thanksgiving?

WEEK 4: WARRIORS
OF GRATITUDE

Day 1

Welcome to the last week! One of the first keys to thankfulness we talked about was acknowledging how great God is and His love for each of us and fully surrendering to His plan over the lives of ourselves and those we love. With this in mind, take a look at 1 Samuel 1:21–2:11 and then come back to this.

What a hero Hannah is in giving her child's life over to the Lord. I love what she says in verse 28 of chapter 1, "So now I give him over to the Lord. For his whole life he will be given over to the Lord."

Hannah knew she would have to continually give Samuel over to God. It was too great a challenge to do one time. She chose to give him over and then she praised God beautifully.

It takes so much courage for us to give the lives of those we love continually over to God, and it also takes so much bravery to then be thankful for whatever calling God has on their lives! Accepting the calling to be Christ's followers, no matter the circumstances, is a major commitment. Remember—He calls us to actively follow Him above everything else that is happening in our lives. Believing in our core that this earth is a temporary home is vital. May we trust in Him; may we seek Him with all we've got so that we will truly be His, no matter the calling He has placed on ourselves and those we love. And may we be thankful; His path and the home He has prepared for us are so much greater than anything or anyone else on our journey!

How is believing that this earth is temporary important in shaping our thankfulness?

What are ways you can make yourself more aware of this? How can you remind yourself of the home that waits for you?

Day 2

Today is a great one! Let's get right into the Word by reading Luke 1:26–38. Take a few minutes to read and then come back.

I hope one big thing we are all noticing is how courageous we are going to have to be to accept and be thankful for the Lord's calling on our lives. If your life does not look like the lives of actors portrayed in commercials, magazines, etc.-—that is a great thing! When we look at heroes like Mary and think about the ways she was probably outcast, called to move through Jesus's young life, the wonder she must have had of Him, the sorrow she must have felt… I hope we are blown away.

God has callings on each and every one of us. They are *not* going to look like a dream or a fairytale—and praise God for that! If you're still committed to being on His journey because you're grateful enough to know that it is the only one that brings true peace, joy, and love in your life and you know without a doubt that even though the path may cost you everything you have on this earth—yet you desire to continue to be on it because you know there is no one like Jesus—go ahead, look in the mirror and say to yourself, "You are a follower!" I certainly think so! I hope you have a wonderful day abiding in Him and being thankful that He sees how brave you are even when you may not!

In what area are you having to be brave right now?

In light of the fact that this is not our permanent home and that we are running to the prize, how does this help your perspective?

In what ways do you think Mary had to truly be brave?

Day 3

Let's go back to 1 Thessalonians 5:16–18: "Be joyful always; pray continually; give thanks in all circumstances, for this is God's will for you in Christ Jesus."

Remember who wrote this under the direction of the Holy Spirit? It was Paul. Paul, formerly Saul, whose resume included wrecking the lives of those following the Lord. Yet we see from these verses that even Paul knew he had the right to be thankful. Isn't it strange how sometimes we tell ourselves we don't really have the right to receive certain gifts of God? It is very important that we put a stop to that thinking because it is a lie. Christ's blood covers all of us and we have the right and access to every gift the Lord has to give.

Pull up the song "So Will I" by Hillsong Worship. One of the most powerful verses I've ever heard in a song is in it and says, "If you left the grave behind you, so will I."

We are freed! What grave do you need to leave behind you so that you can live in thankfulness to our God? If you pay attention to the verses in 1 Thessalonians, this is not just a suggestion but rather God's will for us—that we will live in thanksgiving continually. Leave that grave; it is not yours to stay in! Christ has set us free! Take some time and listen to this beautiful song of praise. I pray you are able to lift up your heart to Him as you listen.

Day 4

I hope your heart is full as we finish this study. Read through the following scriptures in Mark.

> Jesus called them together and said, "You know that those who are regarded as rulers of the Gentiles lord it over them, and their high officials exercise authority over them. Not so with you. Instead, whoever wants to become great among you must be your servant, and whoever wants to be first must be slave of all. For even the Son of Man did not come to be served, but to serve, and to give his life as a ransom for many."
> (Mark 10:42–45)

Christ was the ultimate servant. Last week, we talked about how He beautifully serves those who are in a position in which they cannot help themselves. We also talked about how as Christ's followers this is a key part of our makeup. If we are not doing this, there's going to be a hole that we try to fill, and we may not fill it the right way if we do not realize what it is for. One of my friends put it so well when she said that when we are personally involved in serving those in need and it is part of our regular routine, we can see the love of the Lord that much more. I was very humbled one morning on a mission trip whenever I served scrambled eggs to families undergoing hardships with a woman in her eighties who made that part of her weekly routine. She could have very well decided her days to physically and personally serve others were over, but she did not. There are *so* many places to serve those who cannot help themselves. I wanted to come back to this through looking at the example of Christ one more day before we finish. It is one of the most beautiful blessings I think we can experience in our lives and truly does bring so much gratitude. If you don't have this as part of your regular routine, pray for God to open your eyes, your schedule, and your heart to personally serve those in need. I hope you are blessed today!

What is an area in which you feel you would enjoy serving?

Who do you need to reach out to in order to start?

Spend some time praying for God to open doors for you to be able to serve those in need regularly.

Day 5

One last hello to all of you through this Bible study! Below are some of the main points we have focused on over the past few weeks in our endeavor to grow in gratitude:

- We must understand that our Father is constantly at work in our lives and in the lives of those we love (Psalm 107).
- We must remember that our thoughts of the decisions or the paths those we love should take, are not His.
- One of the best ways to start our day can be to tell the Lord that we are giving our day over to Him and ask to be filled with gratitude.
- The more we choose love over fear throughout each day, the more thankfulness will grow inside of us.
- Working personally with those who cannot help themselves is a natural stimulant for gratitude.
- Having a continual spirit of thankfulness is what God has called us to do.

Choosing gratitude in our lives takes work and courage, remember—you'll be a true follower for it! Thank you so much for allowing me to share what I have learned with you. I pray we are changed for the better from this study. I'll leave you with the beautiful words of Mary from Luke 1:46–55:

And Mary said:

> "My soul glorifies the Lord
> and my spirit rejoices in God my Savior,
> for he has been mindful
> of the humble state of his servant.
> From now on all generations will call me blessed,
> for the Mighty One has done great things for
> me—
> holy is his name.

His mercy extends to those who fear him,
from generation to generation.
He has performed mighty deeds with his arm;
He has scattered those who are proud in their
    inmost thoughts.
He has brought down rulers from their thrones
but has lifted up the humble.
He has filled the hungry with good things
but has sent the rich away empty.
He has helped his servant Israel,
remembering to be merciful
to Abraham and his descendants forever,
just as he promised our ancestors."

May we hold onto thankfulness by the grace of Jesus!

Study Reflection

How do you feel your mindset has been affected by this study in regard to rejoicing? Are there any habits that you have kept since going through those four weeks?

How has your prayer life been affected from the section on prayer?

How do you feel your mind has been affected in regard to giving thanks? What do you want to hold onto from this study?

How do you feel you have changed in general since beginning this study?

What practices do you want to remain a part of your normal routine?

Thank you for completing this study! I pray that you are coming out better on the other side. Remember, rejoicing, praying, and giving thanks are practices God has planned for us. May you be tremendously blessed as you continue on your journey!

ABOUT THE AUTHOR

Katie lives on a farm just south of Montgomery, Alabama. Her wonderful husband and daughter bless her life tremendously. She spends her days as an educator and enjoys being involved in church, writing, reading, and traveling. For her, there is nothing better in this life than relationships with God, family, and friends.